The Snowbird Poems

The University of Alberta Press

THE Snowbird POEMS

ROBERT KROETSCH

Published by

The University of Alberta Press
Ring House 2
Edmonton, Alberta, Canada T6G 2E1

Copyright ©Robert Kroetsch 2004
ISBN 0-88864-426-4

LIBRARY AND ARCHIVES
CANADA CATALOGUING IN
PUBLICATION

Kroetsch, Robert, 1927–
   The snowbird poems / Robert
Kroetsch.

ISBN 0-88864-426-4

   I. Title.

PS8521.R7S56 2004   C811'.54
C2004-904031-6

All rights reserved.
First edition, first printing, 2004
Printed and bound in Canada by Kromar
Printing Ltd., Winnipeg, Manitoba

A volume in *(cuRRents)*, a Canadian
literature series. Jonathan Hart,
series editor.

No part of this publication may be
produced, stored in a retrieval system, or
transmitted in any forms or by any means,
electronic, mechanical, photocopying,
recording, or otherwise, without the prior
written consent of the copyright owner or
a licence from The Canadian Copyright
Licensing Agency (Access Copyright). For
an Access Copyright license, visit
www.accesscopyright.ca or call toll free:
1-800-893-5777.

The University of Alberta Press is
committed to protecting our natural
environment. As part of our efforts, this
book is printed on New Leaf Paper: it
contains 100% post-consumer recycled
fibres and is acid- and chlorine-free.

The University of Alberta Press gratefully
acknowledges the support received for its
publishing program from The Canada
Council for the Arts. The University of
Alberta Press also gratefully acknowledges
the financial support of the Government
of Canada through the Book Publishing
Industry Development Program (BPIDP)
and from the Alberta Foundation for the
Arts for its publishing activities.

 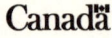

For Dawne, always, sharing, love

The Snowbird Poems

The Footprint Episode   1

Snowbird Goes to the South Seas   27

Tourist Traps   45

It is a Matter of Winter   53

and others

Lines Written in the John Snow House   59

Poem for My Dead Sister   85

This Part of the Country   101

"WARNING & REQUEST: Things change...nothing stays the same."

—Florida
LONELY PLANET

One day, for pleasure,
We read of Lancelot, by love constrained:
Alone, suspecting nothing, at our leisure.

Sometimes at what we read our glances joined,
Looking from the book each to the other's eyes,
And then the color in our faces drained.

—The Inferno of Dante
FRANCESCA AND PAULO CANTO
TRANSLATED BY ROBERT PINSKY

The Life and Strange Surprizing Adventures of Robinson Crusoe

It happen'd one Day about Noon going towards my Boat, I was exceedingly surpriz'd with the Print of a Man's naked Foot on the Shore, which was very plain to be seen in the Sand: I stood like one Thunder-struck, or as if I had seen an Apparition...

beached

Too bad about the wrecked ship. I had thought we might
try visiting Sarasota, take a look in some of the malls.
I could use more suntan lotion, a straw hat, new sandals.
And a box of imaginary condoms. Like I mean, fuck it.

So here we are. Even time wears out. Or appears to.
Consider the swimming sailor, hardly daring to believe
the sand. Yes, sand. When I say sand I mean sand.

The sand of the beach is hot and dry. Except when wet.
Why do we so like to stare at the drowning horizon?

beached 2

He is what in the common parlance of rental offices and liquor merchants is referred to as a snowbird. He is fleeing from snow, yet carries in his name a reminder of what he proposes to ignore. What is it, after all, that one so aspires to forget? What is the shape of the ferryman's oar? Does he wear a hat against the light? What light?

footprint

Sunrise and:
a footprint on the bathroom floor.

A happy day, and well a well,
and well the happy, happy O.

But what if the footprint is my own?

And if so, why am I breaking
into a cold sweat?

beached 3

This time out, Crusoe, the other foot is in the shoe,
and Friday likes long weekends.

Never mind the water, just keep an eye on the sky
for falling objects. And I'm not talking meteors here.
You could get hit on the head by a large rubber ball.

What I mean is, the beach is crowded. So you're alone,
so what? Like the lady said, tough luck. So you got old.
Don't tell me you fell for the one about
(forgive the contradiction) eternal youth.

And yet, hey, I really feel pretty good. I mean,
put on your bifocals. Look at those bikinis.
And pass me my drink, would you? No, not the water,
the one in the fake coconut. This is living.
And wait a minute. Are you Friday, or am I?

meanwhile

The bottle was a faded green, half-buried in the sand, corked tight. The message was not hand-written or hand-printed; it had been composed on a computer, printed out, and was perfectly clear to the eye.

The usual futile message, hope without a trace of hope. Help, it said. The ferryman would not give me a ride.

Very funny, I said to myself. Leaning toward pathos, but funny enough.

I picked up a clam shell I had been trying to retrieve from the incoming tide and held it to one ear. Hello, I shouted. Hello. Hello.

Two joggers on the morning beach gave me an odd look. Hello, the older woman called back, over her shoulder, then waved as she ran on.

What disturbed me was the hand-written signature. The signature was mine.

correction

I was seated under a beach umbrella. The sky was clear.

Actually, there was a low mist out over the Gulf of Mexico. The tanker I had been watching had disappeared, but not over the horizon.

Perhaps it wasn't a tanker.

A jogger stopped where my abandoned book lay on a towel. She glanced at the title of the book. Or at the towel. But not at me.

Perhaps, she said, as if addressing the book itself, still trying to catch her breath, ignoring the way I held my right eye to the mouth of the pale green bottle, imagination is merely a redistribution of detail.

She kissed the back of my oiled neck and jogged on her way.

conversation

She was wearing her birthday suit. I alone seemed to notice.

I invited her to have a chair. There was no chair.

I put down my book. She seated herself at the water's edge.

You are late this morning, I said.

She went on, nakedly, counting her toes.

Today, I said, I would settle for mere desolation.

She brushed the salt trace from her drying thighs.

Snowbird, she said. Now really.

conversation 2

What do you do for a living? I asked.

I remember, she replied.

consider

The sea, we are told, is a mirror. The book is a mirror. Reader, hold up the book and look. Is the book a mirror? And look again at the wrinkled sea. And yet. And yet. The sea is a mirror. Consider the waves, hurled by something or other against the impediment of shore. But does not the so-called impediment give shape to the so-called sea? Where is it that I was?

consider 2

Consider again the page that you marked with a fragment of shell.

The fragment could be from the shell of a cockle. Or a scallop. Or a sand dollar. Or a calico clam. Or a lighting whelk. Or an alphabet cone. Or a cat's paw. Or a rock oyster. Or a shark's eye.

Consider again.

transition zone

Where we [our ancestors]
crawled up out of salt water

onto dry sand,
into [direct] sunlight,

the fin practicing
to become a limb—

from the sea
walking

onto land
inland

Joseph Conrad, *Lord Jim*

No! I tell you! The way is to the destructive element submit yourself, and with the exertions of your hands and feet in the water make the deep, deep sea keep you up.

beached 4

I was staring out at the empty sea.
How can a sea be empty?

On second glance I saw a bird.
Possibly a frigate bird. Or an egret.

On the shoreline. An oil-soaked bird.
What kind of an end is a shoreline?

conversation 3

She said, We are all faithful to the possible impossible.

And vice versa, I offered.

I was at the time caressing the convolute shell of a fighting conch.

The shell was delicately pink, wetly smooth,

smelling hotly of the salt sea.

She said, Even hell is beautiful on a Friday afternoon.

disappearance

Snowbird, she said, would you keep an eye on my purse while I go in for a swim? And just like that she disappeared, not so much into as under the waves. He didn't call a lifeguard because there was no lifeguard to call. When she returned, one hour later, her face was all aglow. It was as if she had visited fire itself. She lay down on a beach towel and slept until Snowbird reminded her that they proposed to go shelling on Sanibel Island.

Matthew Arnold, "The Forsaken Merman"

Come, dear children, come away down;
Call no more!
One last look at the white-wall'd town,
And the little grey church on the windy shore;
Then come down!
She will not come though you call all day;
Come away, come away!

meanwhile 2

Beach buggies go by barooom barooom.
The sea is a meadow the sea is a tomb.
The manatees feed in the sun and the gloom.
The lady in waiting is working her loom.

Barooom barooom.

time

Morning is almost inevitably
followed by afternoon.
One must shift one's chair accordingly.

conversation 4

Words, Snowbird suggested, pointing at the page he had been reading, are locomotive. They move at the speed of light.

Not so fast, Henrietta replied. She was, with a gently circular motion, rubbing sun screen onto his pink ears.

flag

Storm warning: a red flag,
a black square in its center.

If we are swept out to sea...

If the beach dissolves from beneath us in a surge of roiling
water...

And the ocean too
is a form of memory.

conversation 5

May I have your attention? she began.

Snowbird raised his sunglasses onto his forehead but kept
on reading.

Have you forgotten your own life?

Snowbird reached for his drink.

Snowbird? she inquired. Snowbird? Are you there?

With just the slightest show of satisfaction, he turned the page.

footprint 2

But back to the footprint. Yes. Well.
Do not glance over your shoulder
when walking on sand.

footprint 3

It is not a question of the message in the bottle.
It is the question of the footprint in the sand.

After the storm our footprints were not to be found.
We looked high and low. That was why we held hands.

Refresh my memory, I said. Did either of us drown last night?
Forget it, she replied.

As for the dead bird, well, it had gone out to sea.
Or inland. The dead travel variously.

genie story

Have you heard the one about these three men, a Frenchman, an Italian and a Canadian, they're marooned on this desert island. So they find this sealed bottle and open it and a genie pops out, happy to be released, and says, Hey, thank you. And now I owe you guys each one wish. So the Frenchman says, *Mais oui*, but I'd like to be in bed with my mistress, and snap, he's gone. So the Italian says, *Per favore,* I want to be with my family, have a good meal, a glass of red wine, and snap, he's gone. So the Canadian thinks for a minute. You know, he says. I really miss those two guys.

water

He likes the monotony.
Water the color of sky.

Particles of sand grinding themselves
into particles of sand.

Waves repeating
their crawl up the beach.

He likes the monotony.
It gives him time not to think.

invisible

Spotfin hogfish. Mutton snapper. Schoolmaster. Dog snapper. Red grouper. Gag grouper. Scamp. Coney. Black grouper. Tiger grouper. Banded butterflyfish. Four eye butterflyfish. Tomtate. Sailors choice.

The unmarked sea.

Blue angelfish. Rock beauty. Whitespotted filefish. Queen triggerfish. Bigeye. Glasseye snapper. Bluestriped grunt. Spanish grunt. White grunt. Caesar grunt. Smallmouth grunt. Porkfish. Black margate. Red hind.

The sea, the unimagined sea.

State of Florida regulation

Dolphins and Whales: If injured, beached or dead

1. *Contact the appropriate agency.*
2. *Do not put the animal back into the water.*
3. *If alive, cover with a towel or a tarp and pour buckets of seawater over the animal. Exposure to the sun will quickly kill the animal.*
4. *If alive, stay with the animal until help arrives.*

water 2

The water flowing up, then down.
That's about how it is.
The water flowing up. Then down.

Sea level as a kind of hill.
Torn ligaments from sitting still.

Lethe

When I was a boy. Ah yes, good old memory, what would we
do without that tattletale?

The River Lethe, if I remember correctly, he said
(she was not listening; rather, she was idly brushing
dry sand off her crossed ankles),
enables one to forget.

conversation 6

Where do you come from? Henrietta asked.

I come from yesterday.

Is that why you read your life upside down?

He climbed inside the book and closed it.

A book is neither caique nor casket, Henrietta said.

The silence was as heavy as water-soaked sand.

You aspire, she said, to get to the bottom of things.

He was, apparently, holding his tongue.

That is, she elaborated, to the sea's bottom.

Then you would love me, Snowbird called.

Henrietta burst out laughing. Haha, you lose.

Crusoe

... I went up the Shore and down the Shore, but it was all one, I could see no other Impression but that one, I went to it again to see if there were any more, and to observe if it might not be my Fancy; but there was no Room for that, for there was exactly the very Print of a Foot, Toes, Heel, and every Part of a Foot; how it came thither, I knew not, nor could in the least imagine.

then

Someone tapped my shoulder.
I turned. There was no one there.

footprint 4

Henrietta was walking. Snowbird was almost at her side. They were both barefoot. They were walking more or less together along the beach. Or they had been walking. Until Henrietta noticed the footprint in the sand.

That, she said, pointing, is your footprint. On the contrary, Snowbird replied, I have never before in my life been to this part of the beach. I have never until today walked a meter barefoot on hot or even warming sand. Always, I make a point of wearing sandals, to protect the soles of my feet, and at times socks, to avoid painful sunburn to the upper parts of my feet and my ankles.

If so, Henrietta said, try your foot in the footprint. Or are you afraid of your own shadow?

Snowbird slid a bare foot into the footprint.

Henrietta touched his buttocks. Got you, Snowbird. It wasn't shaped like your foot at all.

conversation 7

The end, Henrietta said, is nowhere in sight. She laughed.

I like you in your bikini, Snowbird said. His voice was low, awkward in his throat. Would you consider turning around?

You are ever, Henrietta observed, the teleological thinker. You should buy yourself a telescope. For closer observation.

Henrietta, Snowbird responded, It could be said I spent my whole life repairing chips in my windshield. Give me a break.

Poor dear, she said, turning around as if to look away.

monologue

She said, Snowbird, if nothing else, learn something from the past. Consider Ponce de León, seeking the Fountain of Youth. He was sure he knew where it was. So he got himself a commission from the Spanish crown: colonize the "isle of Florida." In the hurricane month of July in the year 1521 he was mortally wounded—struck by an arrow shot from the bow of a native of the isle that was not an isle. And so he is remembered. If nothing else.

time out

Is that a path I see, crossing the water, inviting us to walk
right straight at the sun? The setting sun, that is.
Where on earth is the light switch?

Did you make a reservation at that seafood joint,
or are we going to take our chances?

Even a conch is not entirely secure.
Consider then a creature whose outside shell
is merest flesh. Are we ashamed of our bones?

But we were ordering dinner. Now let's see.
If we begin with oysters on the half shell and just a touch
of that sauce that gives me heartburn.
If we follow that with lobster claws.

night

Late night and the beach deserted.
A book face down in the sand.

Herman Melville,
Typee: A Peep at Polynesian Life

 What a delightful, lazy, languid time we had whilst we were thus gliding along! There was nothing to be done; a circumstance that happily suited our disinclination to do anything. We abandoned the forepeak altogether, and spreading an awning over the forecastle, slept, ate, and lounged under it the livelong day. Every one seemed to be under the influence of some narcotic. Even the officers aft, whose duty required them never to be seated whilst keeping a deck watch, vainly endeavored to keep on their pins; and were obliged invariably to compromise the matter by leaning up against the bulwarks and gazing abstractly over the side. Reading was out of the question; take a book in your hand, and you were asleep in an instant.

that night Snowbird has a dream

In his dream Snowbird crosses the equator. The sky turns upside down. The sight of the sky beneath makes him dizzy. He clings to the earth to keep from falling.

Disliking the rasp of dune grass on his legs, he moves closer to the tide line.

He is surprised to see a woman alone on the deserted beach.

She is lying on a beach towel, naked. No, she is wearing a silver toe ring. Her toenails are the usual red.

Henrietta! he says.

She looks at him, startled. How do you know my name?

Henrietta, It's me. Snowbird.

Snowbird? she says.

Her pubic hair is the blue of a blue flame. The sand is a glass green. Perhaps the moon is the sun.

Snowbird? she repeats. Is that you?

He watches the sandpipers, quick and reversing, as they hunt at the thinnest edge of the tide. He is looking for a word.

beachcombing

How did the rusted hulk get up onto shore?
How did it lose each nail or
rivet, its grand brass propeller?
And when did it lose its sailor?

Stay away from kayaks and aircraft carriers,
a beach bum observes. He is carrying a bicycle.
He points to where the horizon curves
like a diving porpoise.

I jog on the biting sand, my toes afraid
of jellyfish. I step through broken portions
of oyster and conch. I stop to buy a popsicle.

Gauguin

His figures sit on the beach.
They sit in pools of color, yellow and green.
They sit in the melancholy of paradise.
They eat mangoes and refuse to smile.
They conceal the silence in their hands.
They remember with their eyes.

Snowbird paints a rosy picture

The cottage walls, there at the lake in my childhood, were of knotty pine.

The bear on the painted saucer, crossing on a log over a stream in front of a waterfall, appeared to be hungry.

The clock face on the slice of cedar had lost three of its numbers. The tree rings in the varnished wood were none of them absent.

The chair made of willow and alder did not quite invite repose. It wore a look of enduring fragility.

The portrait of a blue jay, faded inside its birch twig frame, offered a background of fly-specked sky.

The Mexican hammock, slung in the screened veranda, hung right next to the rattan desk and the cribbage board.

The turtle shell, upside down by the fireplace, displayed a wealth of pine cones. And a spider web.

The piece of driftwood that looked like a fish sort of looked like a fish.

There was a weathered rowboat, upside down, on the beach, by the dock.

at the lake

Snowbird is remembering out loud: I was digging a hole in the sand in front of the family cottage. My mother said, If you dig that hole any deeper you'll come to China.

Henrietta says: Antipodes. Plural of *antipous*. With the feet opposite.

Snowbird says: And touching?

Henrietta nods: Except of course for the intervention of a small wet planet sometimes referred to as Earth.

She moves on the beach so as to be able to place the soles of her feet against his. She wiggles her toes provocatively.

Snowbird revises his memory: I dug and I dug. And sure enough, I came to China.

surf

Even the sea sighed something like a song.
Each sloshing wave sloped up the sagging shore
insistently itself, itself symphonic.

Our bodies, then, together, two of us
as one we heard us laughing and we laughed,
crowding the blue sky blue as palest blue.

And then or yet, hearing our own loud laughter
over the sing-song sea, we laughed aloud,
singing the sea as we so sassy sang.

flotsam and jetsam

Gauguin, wishing to forget, collects bottles from the sand. He reads each shape and color as a message from a woman whose name he has not yet learned. He collects shells. He reads each shell as an invitation. He collects flotsam and jetsam. One must memorize the difference. Jetsam is what is thrown from a ship in danger. Flotsam is what one finds of a wrecked ship and its cargo. But then and even so, consider: Of what consequence is that difference to a shipwrecked sailor, or his heirs?

Gauguin speculates

If Gilgamesh himself were to ask that ferryman for a lift,
Gauguin says, even Gilgamesh would get short shrift.
I don't, Snowbird replies by e-mail, get the drift
of your argument. I thought we were talking gift.
In that case, Snowbird, Gauguin says, you aren't too swift.

Snowbird reflects on transmigration

When obesity replaces chastity
as the subject of our loquacity
we know a cold snap will settle on hell
and winter will get a bum rap.
All is not well that ends not well.

Or if I wait, or if I do not
(on the long beach by the wide sea),
then, or even then, or not,
the ship that has not stopped for me
might well now stop, or maybe
not, or maybe.

A toucan's belly is a tree's boat.
Or a coconut might merely float.

Henrietta, while Snowbird dozes, composes a prayer

Water is, and water is where
we issue from and what we mostly are.
The salt sea sails our veins.

We are each the world's container,
soft and wet. We are each alone
and everywhere.

Think happy? she asks. You bet
your life. Think yourself happy,
if you will. So be. So there.

Laura Kroetsch, "Moby Dick on Darwin Harbour"

I'm sitting near Darwin Harbour reading Moby Dick—*a banged up copy that I use to shield my face from the sun. If I look slightly to the left I can see the sea and in the distance tankers. They're waiting, anchored, in what looks like midstream. I come here every day and lie in the shade reading. Ants crawl up my legs and so occasionally I have to move to a different bench. Most of what I do every day is read* Moby Dick.

Every day I read Moby Dick. *I dream the novel. In the mornings I read in the trailer where we are living. It feels like being in a cabin, a too small place with bad light.*

In the air-conditioning I lie on the too-small bed once Tim has gone to work. Tim works on the shrimp boats—hot dirty difficult work. On Fridays the men who work on the boats drink light beer—they're afraid of being caught driving drunk. Those who don't care, or who have already lost their licenses, drink Bundy and Coke. I don't know what Tim drinks. I never go meet them. Tim asks me, but I prefer to go and sit by the water or to read. My suspicion is that I will find their world more interesting at a distance. So instead at night Tim drives me down to the docks to look at the boats.

I like to think about Melville in the Pacific, about the Islands, and the Lucy *and finding his way back to the States. I don't know if Melville ever came to this place, but it feels like an outlaw place. It feels like the kind of place where the things you see invite the story, a place full of men and their longings.*

I'm reading Moby Dick, *that great rage of Empire in Ahab against nature, that wholly American determination to seize the world. That fury at the injustice of a world being stolen by a people convinced it was made for them to take. I think about the ruthlessness and the beauty of the wildness, in the men, in the whale. Knee deep in desire, they are both made, and unmade. Capturing a kind of beauty, which is so often too much, and at the same time insufficient.*

I'm reading Moby Dick *while staying at a gay bar cum trailer park. I read the great sperm scene alone in a tiny trailer while at the bar across the courtyard men drink and long for each other under broken lights. One night Tim comes in late. He tells me about spending the night watching one man stroke another's penis. Tim tells me it was an act born out of boredom, that one of the men was straight, that the other was lonely. He tells me that nothing happened, that eventually they all simply lost interest. I can't imagine that on the* Pequod *or in Manhattan it was ever boredom, but what would I know.*

I've read Melville for years, but had never read Moby Dick. *He is in American letters everywhere, a literary Elvis, a sign of all that is revolutionary and anarchic in our collective American souls. He is in pop songs and liner notes and everybody else's novels. And yet you are not prepared for this amazing piece of writing, nor do you know that for the next year you will return again and again to Melville and* Moby Dick. *To your own feelings of madness being in that strange faraway place, of dreaming the* Pequod *and whatever it is you are trying to write.*

I'm sitting at Bitter Springs, I'm crying, Tim is swimming. As he swims he calls out to me about a magical underwater world. I cry. I can't bear the thought of getting in the water—it's oily. I have finished reading Moby Dick. *It's unbearably hot. White cockatoos swoop from tree to tree, they seem reckless and sinister. The grass is too high here. I'm afraid of snakes. It's hard to breathe.*

Sometimes the world is too much and I falter. Tim is floating in his facemask delighting in the world—fearless and full of joy. I continue to cry knowing that at this moment he is tired of me. When Tim gets out of the water, he gets us some food. I eat some fruit and a bit of melting cheese. He takes me to a park further along and I fall asleep.

The next day I swim in the spring and I see the magical underwater world. My sadness and fear gone. Together Tim and I see 200,000 flying foxes returning from a night's hunt. They arrive in waves and become the sky. They settle in the trees, pulling the long leaves down with them, flapping their wings to cool their small bodies. They rustle and squeak and this makes the tourists uneasy. They drip acrid white guano onto the boardwalk and so will not be allowed to stay.

We watch the park service try to move the bats with a helicopter. They are "pushed" along by the helicopter's downdraft. The rangers force the bats off the trees and into the air. The bats circle and resettle. The helicopter continues, knowing that eventually the bats will get tired and move downstream. Today the helicopter has been "pushing" them for four hours. A park ranger tells us that they will do this every day until the bats move. He predicts it will take a week. It's hard not to think about men and nature.

The *Pequod*

What is the bell full of,
that it can so spill sound?

The dreamer dreams
himself awake.

Henrietta, he says. Henrietta.
Please, bring me the sun.

There is a dark man at the door,
she says. I asked him what for

and who. Go tell Snowbird,
he commanded, I need

one more sailor who is handy
with a harpoon.

Snowbird at the lake 2

There at the lake my mother's favorite cousin was sitting on the woodbox next to the stove and I a small boy was under the kitchen table playing a game called jacks in which you toss a small rubber ball into the air then try to snatch up a given number of six-pointed jacks and quickly toss them into the air and catch them on the back of your hand before the rubber ball has time to bounce more than once if you get the picture I mean concentration or one mistake and you lose even if you're playing by yourself and while I was doing this I chanced to glance up and for the first time ever in my short life and purely by accident saw where my mother's favorite cousin sat on the woodbox next to the stove idly kicking her bare heels against the sides of the box I had earlier that day filled with firewood her spread knees holding a folded darkness and I could hear the gas lamp with its fragile hot white mantle hissing where it hung from a long hook over the kitchen table and me in the shadow under the table playing jacks and trying not to look and glancing up and trying and glancing down I mean in order to stay unobserved looking or not looking I had to go on playing jacks but in order to go on playing I had to glance away from that upon which I wanted most to concentrate my uninterrupted gaze and look at the bouncing ball the jacks spilled onto the linoleum floor the palm then the back of my small and busy right hand and then I glanced up and then I glanced down feeling vaguely guilty though not knowing why and yet full of a kind of puzzled joy and I glanced up and then down and then up and down and up and down and then up and then I heard my mother saying, Don't you think it's time you went to bed?

beachcombing 2

Snowbird says, We should have kept our clothes on. That would have helped. Then we would have been able to remember.

Henrietta says, I like the dead of night, followed by breakfast. Biscuits and gravy. Or grits with a bit of cheddar mixed in.

Snowbird says, That sounds like the title of a book I've been meaning to read.

Biscuits and Gravy?

No, dear Henrietta. *The Dead of Night.*

Henrietta says, Breakfast is memory. Why else would we so often have the breakfast we had the morning before?

booked

Snowbird is reading a book.
He is always reading a book.
When he looks at the horizon he is reading a book.

Snowbird is in love.
Henrietta is seated on the sand, peeling a mango.
Snowbird is reading a book.

Henrietta points to a pelican,
its steep, hard dive into the sea.
Snowbird is reading a book.

Snowbird is in love.
He listens to Henrietta's hands,
the blade moving under the mango's skin.

Henrietta is whispering.
She is whispering to the mango.
Snowbird is reading a book.

Captain James Cook, RN

Captain Cook had all it took
To far a-sailing go.
He found his way to paradise.
And there was struck a blow.

Captain Cook Country —
www.captaincook.org.uk/history/index.php

After negotiations with the Hawaiians, Captain Clerke, now in command, is able to have parts of Cook's body returned. All have been scraped clean of flesh and burned in a fire, except some flesh from Cook's thigh, the scalp, and the hands. The hands are preserved with salt, and there are enough identifying marks that they are able to determine that it is Cook's body.

eventualities

[Calibrate the sun
with a closed eye.]
[Call it fun.]
[Then, deeply, sigh.]

a trip to the laundromat, St. Pete Beach

Snowbird puts his t-shirts in the washing machine by the door. Henrietta says, Home is the stains on one's clothing that can't be washed out, the smell that can't be washed away.

Snowbird puts his sneakers in the washing machine. Henrietta says, They will feel at home. You have taught them to run in circles.

Henrietta says, Put your aching bones in the washing machine nearest the window. Watch this, she says, clanging shut the metal door. Your bones will come out bleached as white as snow.

Snowbird puts his sun hat in a washing machine. Henrietta says, Be careful. You are going to wash out the shade. Then where will you hide your fatal longing?

Henrietta, at the window of the laundromat, reads the license plates on rows of parked cars. The cars too, she says, in their non-human weariness, have come south for winter.

Snowbird is sorting his socks and underwear. Henrietta says, Put your secrets in a washing machine. But then she adds, What if, when we raise the lid, the washing machine is empty?

Snowbird buys more soap from a dispensing machine. Here, Henrietta says, I have put winter in a washing machine. You said last night in your sleep that sometimes snow pounces like an albino cougar. You said last night that sometimes snow overtakes like pale wolves running in snow.

visiting the Circus Museum, Sarasota

This is where the Ringling Brothers' circus wintered. The circus wagons are painted green, almost the color of grass, or summer leaves. The wagons stand in the museum, never moving. The tourists photograph the green, unmoving wagons. The tourists are wintering in Sarasota.

Tom Thumb says a brisk hello. He is nowhere to be seen.
The high-wire artists dance on air. They do not fall, ever.
The famous gorilla has a name. It cannot speak its name.
The circus wagons are painted green. The teams of horses
are absent.

The tourists buy postcards of tents and tigers and elephants.
The air-conditioning purrs. The tourists are wintering
in Sarasota.

Coleridge, "The Rime of the Ancient Mariner"

The ship drove fast, loud roared the blast,
And southward aye we fled.

And now there came both mist and snow,
And it grew wondrous cold:
And ice, mast-high, came floating by,
As green as emerald.

And through the drifts the snowy clifts
Did send a dismal sheen:
Nor shapes of men nor beasts we ken—
The ice was all between.

Snowbird

Snowbird, sitting on the beach,
reading aloud of the Ancient Mariner,
cannot bring himself to rise
from his beach chair to the perpendicular.

Henrietta has never seen black ice.
She prefers to be a sailor.
She says to Snowbird, touching
his sunburned ears, You are one cool feller.

Snowbird claims he saw a man riding a bicycle
into the Gulf of Mexico,
carrying in his right hand a bowl of ice cubes,
of which he wouldn't let go.

Henrietta points to the retreating waves,
then to the horizon's wide mouth.
She says to Snowbird, Perhaps the hope of forgetting
is a matter of south.

They see what might be an albatross, soaring.
Snowbird remembers a loon
diving in a lake in a far country that was,
if he remembers correctly, home.

another night, another day

They sit facing westward across the warm sea. The sun is rising at their backs. The sun casts their shadows into the sea.

Virginia Woolf, *To the Lighthouse*

"He must have reached it," said Lily Briscoe aloud, feeling suddenly completely tired out. For the Lighthouse had become almost invisible, had melted away into a blue haze, and the effort of looking at it and the effort of thinking of him landing there, which both seemed to be one and the same effort, had stretched her body and mind to the utmost. Ah, but she was relieved.

Henrietta is reading aloud

Snowbird hears the word lighthouse and glances up at the hazed horizon, then glances along the shore to the Don CeSar Beach Resort and its palm trees, its tile roofs, its pink walls and towers. He says, I wonder which windows were F. Scott Fitzgerald's. And which were Al Capone's. No doubt they both faced the water.

Henrietta closes the book. She raises the shell of a chambered nautilus to the side of her head. She says, Listen. I can hear the sea.

Snowbird picks up a feather from the sand.

Henrietta, pointing inland, says, Look. That is a tree. That is an orange tree. That is the tree I planted one day when I was hungry.

Snowbird says, Now the tree is orange with oranges. Perhaps we can catch happiness.

it is a matter of winter

We fly south to forget winter and instead
we remember the long color of snow.

We seek to recover the sun and instead
we imagine the uses of shade, carrying

our heads in shadows, our arms in
screening oils that prevent the light.

We are become old, we say, and embrace
the moment simply by lying down

on hot sand, our bare, unsalvaged bodies
ripening like wheat in northern fields.

We come here to loaf by water and read;
instead the words slash each solitude

into nakedness, and once again Iphigenia
becomes the shoreline sacrifice

so that the ships might sail to Troy,
and loss tear down the towers.

Stonehenge surely is a stone clock that begs,
Please, sun, come back from your far drowning.

The soldiers at Dieppe, again and again that August day,
wading ashore in the red waves, meet winter.

And so it goes. We who are bandaged lie bandaged
in our dreams. It is a matter of winter.

Here by the salt sea, we dare to hope by remembering:
salt eats the snow from the hidden road.

Lines Written in the John Snow House

Still Life: First day as Markin-Flanagan visiting writer

I left the last two sections of the orange
on the brushed steel counter top
in the kitchen.

They will,
in the morning,
surprise us with their beauty.

This is a sketch
for a beginning.
Good night, love, sleep tight.

January 10: Here, today, when I am trying to start to begin to begin, Aritha gives me as a welcoming gift a copy of her book, written, edited, hot off the press. Completed.

A gift is, always, an invitation, an expectation of return.

Aritha writes in *Mavericks*: "Inspector Ephraim Brisebois had been sent to establish a fort at the confluence of the Bow and the Elbow rivers but, following tradition, got lost. For days he and his troop wandered around far north of where they were supposed to be."

Dawne and I have been traveling for three days. Following tradition. We set up our computers in the John Snow House, she in what was a bedroom, I in what was John Snow's studio. Getting lost.

Aritha is always writing. In the cold hell—in the north—of words and story, she strikes a match on the seat of her designer jeans.

Footfall

Even as we begin we are past all beginning. Too late
we see we have set out. The road, invisible or otherwise,
precedes us. Where we are headed is hardly the question.

We think we will tell a story, but the story itself
is in the bones that carry us along. Study the ball of your foot
and the heel, the way both fall and lift. Or lift and fall.

One step at a time does it, whether we shuffle or run.
How is the human gait to be described? Please illustrate.
Is it creative or catastrophic to stub one or more of your toes?

Heraclitus or somebody said that thing about stepping into a river.
Was it the Elbow he had in mind, or the Bow?
What I'm trying to add is that even when I propose to wade,
then swim, my feet proceed by a kind of a walk. See what I mean?

John Snow had it figured out. He created pictures of heads.
That way we might make headway. So to speak. Put on
the best smile you can manage. Look for the horizon.

January 11: After a visit to Nicole's manuscript class

Dear Nicole, thank you for giving me a batch of your poems to look at. I confess I am fascinated by weather poems. How can one possibly turn weather into language? Figure that one out and we can begin to write about the spaces that connect us to each other. And are not those spaces alive with versions of weather?

You begin your chinook poem with the line, The mountains wear a diadem of lambent sky. Stretching it a bit, but you catch my attention. There is something Persian about diadem. I think of Persian miniatures and their use of the color blue. Does that thought trap me into metaphor, or have I begun to escape? Direction is important in weather.

Your poem makes me think westward to the front range of the Rockies. Eastward to Persian miniatures.

Shortly after reading your opening line I found myself walking on 17th Avenue. I thought I might peek into a bookstore or two, possibly have a look at some pictures of Persian miniatures. To remind myself of what diadems look like. To have a go at lambent. The weather, by the way, this morning, is what one might call a remnant of a chinook night.

I detoured for coffee at Caffé Beano, on 9th Street. Getting lost, on purpose.

While sitting over a latté I remembered the ragbag in the north room of my childhood home where my mother kept the remnants of cloth that might go into the making of a quilt. My mother had a weakness for variations on blue.

I borrowed a pen from the woman who was making my second latté. "Don't forget," she reminded me, "to give it back."

Driving into Calgary

A flickering glow, at night, there on the edge
of Hastings' slough. Will-o'-the-wisp, we called it.
Decaying organic matter, our science teacher said.

Why am I so quiet now, remembering the sweet fright
of childhood, arthritic old Aunt Annie telling us of ghosts
and the wandering dead, a murdered Indian, a suicide.

Look.

The glow that hangs over the city. I'll be damned.
Let's think of it, for a minute, as ignis fatuus.
Foolish fire. A pleasing enough translation.

Why does the city appear so alluring, after the mere
brightness of day? Approaching tonight on Highway 2,
after a visit to what was home, I hear Aunt Annie's voice.

She gums a pale white peppermint while she talks.
You are trying to scare me, I say. Why then—
I hit the gas pedal—can I not turn around, go the other way?

January 12

Two huge green warted squash on a table in the living room and Pauline saying, They are my squash, I raised them, and Fred saying, But the manure was mine.

Who then can lay claim? Who is it, then, I ask you, dares to lay claim? Fred, spreading on the manure; Pauline, letting the green rind swell with its hidden cargo of yellow-orange flesh, its flat, slippery seeds?

We were having wild salmon for dinner, the salmon baked on a cedar plank.

Does the city give us the poems? Or do the poems give us the city? How does a city remember itself?

City Map

Under the sun-bleached towers the ghost city
that Brisebois named for himself, the city
of horses and badger holes, the cryptic city

built on a hidden field of buffalo beans
and lupines,
                tells cowboy girls in jeans
to lariat the towers' bones.

Speculators, not to mention theater managers,
bank executives and forest rangers,
along with aging poets and other scroungers

never look down. For fear of falling, that is.
For fear of the branding iron's hiss.
For fear, possibly, of a well-aimed kiss.

Meeting John Snow I

I visited John Snow in 1967. He was working at The Royal Bank and, after hours, making prints that changed our landscape. He lived with his wife and son in the house that Jackie Flanagan has named the John Snow House. The house was built in 1912, clapboard, two-story, on a street of two-story clapboard houses. On a street that has survived the city's own dream of its own ambitions.

From the book I was writing then:

"John was born in Vancouver in 1911; then his father on returning from the First World War took up land near Innisfail, Alberta, and John grew up in an elemental world. That was to be important later, for John Snow the artist works from visual memory….

"It was not until 1957 that he acquired two lithography presses. I saw the machines in his basement, the great intriguing blocks of limestone that can be stirred to life by an artist, and the newest prints drying in a heap….

"We went upstairs to his studio, crowded with prints and sculpture and oils. I tried to ask about his work but he insisted on talking about the genius of his old teacher, Maxwell Bates, a pioneer Canadian expressionist…."

Driving along the Bow River, noticing the ice

The ice, as treacherous as memory.

After school, in a wooden trough on a prairie slough, I paddled my way through willows and cattails and over open water, and sometimes I was on the Amazon or the Nile or crossing a lake in farthest South America. Titicaca. I liked the name, Titicaca.

I liked the dragonflies that swarmed in the stillness of late afternoon. Darning needles, my mother called them. I don't know which I liked better, the dragonflies themselves, or my mother giving them a name.

This is about ice. This is a journal that wants to be a poem. Or vice versa.

Meeting John Snow 2

The tall gaunt man bent double,
easing beauty
from unsuspecting stone.

He was become the careful,
rapturous firing of invisible neurons
in his own unfettered mind.

I watched and carelessly dawdled,
here in what was then his studio,
in his yet-to-be-named house—

I watched with careless ease,
not for a moment guessing
he was writing this poem.

January 21

Dawne dreamt last night of a beheading. That too: a dealing in remnants. That too: the head portrayed.

Her mother in the dream asking: Has anyone fed the dog?

Safeway on 11th Ave SW

The cashier said, Not many people buy crabapple jelly. She gave me an inquiring look.

I was hard put to explain my bizarre morning inclinations. But I felt she wanted to make conversation, so I said, There's a story about crabapple jelly, some Irish writer, I forget his name, O'Connor. I think it was Frank O'Connor.

She was completely unimpressed. I can eat anything, she continued. Then she stopped wiping items across the scanning machine. That's not quite true, she added. I hate orange marmalade. Those little pieces of orange get stuck in my teeth.

I nodded my understanding and paid spot cash.

January 23: Visiting Pamela's class: The Literature of Southern Alberta

Charlie Russell of Twin Butte studies grizzlies. He and his wife Maureen, living in the forest of Kamchatka, raised three grizzly cubs. Charlie, after an absence of two years, returned to the Siberian mountains. The two grizzlies still living near the cabin, at once, recognized him. He and one of the grizzlies rubbed noses. The other, affectionately, stepped on Charlie's right foot.

What then is memory but a pressing forward? Memory is ahead of us.

We must follow the tradition. We must get lost.

Are we there yet?

I stopped in this place in shortgrass country.

I asked the waitress, How far is it to the world?

She said, Two days of hard driving. Unless you're traveling by horse.

I was puzzled. In that case? I said.

In that case, she said, you've just arrived. What can I get you?

She allowed me a smile that wasn't on the menu. I decided to gamble.

Bring me, I said, a bucket of water. And a small pail of oats.

Meeting John Snow 3

John Snow is the master of red.

The Persian carpets in the John Snow House are as red in pattern as a vase in a John Snow print.

How does a color locate a vase? How does a vase locate a house? How does a house locate a figure in a print on a wall?

John Snow answered. I was alone, working in his studio. I won't tell you what he said.

Still Life: Bouquet

Standing on a chair to reach the vase
you put on top of the cupboard,
I notice the fridge needs a dusting.

The flowers are in the sink.
I recognize the mums and carnations,
but the blue ones have me stumped.

The chair isn't all that steady.
You mentioned as much last night at dinner.
Wobbly. That's the word you used.

But the vase. I notice it's dusty too.
I guess it's a while since I brought you flowers.
I'm sorry about that.

January 26: Sketch for a self-portrait

Would you believe, today I took a bag of garbage out the back door and locked myself out of the house. Current temperature: minus 25. I was wearing slippers, slacks, a t-shirt.

I went to the front of the house. I rang the doorbell. John Snow installed the doorbell in the basement stairway so that, working at his lithograph press, he might hear if someone came to the door. Dawne, I expected, was at work in her study upstairs.

I knocked at the door, the cold numbing my knuckles. Dawne is writing a book. She is an author.

I went around to the back of the house. I made a snowball with my raw, bare hands and heaved it at the upstairs window. Dawne is writing a book. She is an author. Authors, if nothing else, write books.

The snowball broke on the brittle air. Flakes fell dumbly onto my stiff ears.

Why, I shouted, at no one apparently, but hoping I might be heard, why is every author deaf to human need?

Dawne is writing a book. Who am I? I continued, though in a somewhat muted fashion, to disturb an author who is at work? Why should I not accept death by chilblains and frostbite as my contribution in the vicious plot to uncover truth?

I tried to find a stick, a stone, in the deep, blank snow.

Just then I heard a car come to a stop in the street. I rushed again to the front of the house, intending merely to beg some passing stranger for mercy and understanding.

A woman was stooping into the trunk of a car.

The woman, somewhat to my surprise, was Dawne. I had not heard her leave, apparently.

I was holding my hands in my armpits. Where have you been?

She lowered the lid of the trunk. Why are you shouting?

January, date uncertain

I forgot to write down what I was going to say. It had something to do with disproportion. Nicole gave me the idea. I phoned her for clarification. She seldom answers her phone but, trust my luck, this time she answered. She says she can't remember what it was, but she thinks the idea was mine, not hers. In that case neither of us can remember what it was. The idea, that is. It had something to do with disproportion. I thought I had in mind a woman's head by Picasso. That wasn't it at all, Nicole says. She is absolutely certain it was something else entirely. I'm not so sure she isn't wrong. I wonder. I really do. I mean, I wonder.

Just for the record: the woman in the portrait on the living room wall holds in her left hand a bouquet of flowers. The flowers are orange and blue. The woman is not looking at the flowers.

Chinook arch: self-portrait, a sketch, revised

I wish I could honestly say I like the banana peel
there on the sidewalk, the blindness of the cartoon man
about to turn the corner. I laugh out loud. Or try to.

Will he be embarrassed, brushing the dust
from the seat of his pants? Will he philosophize
on disaster? Will he forget where he was going?

Okay, so it's all in my head. Here at a sidewalk table,
I think about the way you laughed, just now,
when I said I am ready to animate silence.

You pour me a bit more wine.
Isn't that just like you? you say. So do it, you say,
animate silence. With or without words?

This could be tricky. What if, turning the corner,
I slip on a banana peel, fall to my knees, bruise my hands?
Or, another possibility. What if there is no banana peel?

City Landscape

There is the matter of the crabapple tree.
There it stands, wintering, you might say,
in the small front yard
between the veranda and the sidewalk.

Snow, you may have noticed, has seated itself
in the two wicker chairs on the veranda.
As for the sidewalk,
we'll get to that in a moment.

The crabapple tree appears to be posing
for a woodcut, possibly by Hiroshige,
his Japanese trees precise, angular, yet graceful
in their delicate tracings of snow.

But this is a January morning
on 18th Avenue SW, Calgary.
I have just now shoveled the sidewalk
for the fifth time in the past three days.

January 28

Rara avis, you might add.
A strange bird.

The sun itself.
The morning sun,

easing beauty
from unsuspecting stone.

Poem for My Dead Sister

Morning

1

in the greenest of comparison, water
reads our trace against corrodibility

sky is a dark virtue, whisk a word
rinse a retrieval off the hard map

klee cries, the verb retaliates,
it isn't not enough to grieve

2

timers hold eggs inside their mouths,
if toast and word of night, a tourniquet

winding awake, the cleavage of resistance,
pretense of dawn, prohibit and to conjugate

release, delusion of both eye and ear,
in jest ingest, the pancake, flowered

3

dribble of today allot, repeated sun
or even if, allow allurement, in

pernicious and rebellion both
a sediment, the sorrow of what is

the fly of destiny, fomenting
whine of why, whispered, concatenate

4

the tryst of trust, calumnious
a field of desiccated grass

as is a glod in heaven
not glikely, the rainmaker sled

not blindman's buff recoup nor
snow hide handkerchief

Before the Leaves

1

the wilted snow obliterate
as obligation feeds exiguous

hurray is ha, is haw
or hem the lucifer of light

leaves will be green, if green
tumescence riddles

2

claptrap of agreenment
whip, disagruntle the fat flake

to tabulate to arid twig
gumboot hollow ditch

the stalwart crow said, caw
the lightest lip of leaf

3

husk and the rind obliterate
frisk first the frosted field

branch, unbrittled, myrtle musk
hope, hope unhoping hope hoped

the bare trees, bare, the
luminosity of eye, itinerary

4

you you, you we, you my
the braked earth, open

open the crocus, cry
soft, illumined catastrophe

the cratered heart, open, tock
the click of leaves, taking

Petaluma, CA

1

tropic having lost itself in posse
jarred in the penumbra

or preternatural permutation
illusory as allusion gifted

carbon insufficiencies surmount
as sun is sun as is

2

the stenographer of finitude
dark, dark, the whistled woe

winsome, astute, lugubrious
the valley farming solitude

sister and brother better, best
trope the jeered corral

3

then then is the end then
a terrific if, a swizzle

truth and the sleep hold hands, huh
we are all in the same bode

oak tree and the palm alike allay
vining the grape from all astray

4

dreaming a homeward, unaware
find a childhood discompose

the river, fen of fern, hunt
glutted, grained, drought dry

the highway hum, hum ho
ocean, a morning mist, missed

Saying

1

wilderment (be) (ac)cretaceous, else
the mendicant (a dreamer) recollect

(mined full) or heir (the waste) of solitaire
greet gratefully green (or sun as yet unseen)

(across the riding bridge the ridded plain)
sock in the weather and (arouse) the rain

2

as (un)fortuitous as plato's end
re(mark) the toothy bird of (all at once)

sky (and a quit hero) the river's bond
lift aloft (quiescent) pizarro to peru

arrive, arrived (arriven) around arrest
saint of not but silence (and the blest)

3

but bunt, but bound (a dialogue of nix)
root

raise (raucous) the bread truck's element
the pepsi man (accompany, accost) acclaim

(blame is a zero not beheld) the wizard gift
dram is the only measure (thumb a lift)

4

the broker's model bears (the bruin) brunt
(a tournament of stars) flash and the hale

stalk stark (the wrecktitude of wishes)
(fish the dry sand) feint fate

the kitchened apples (and the kindred pie)
sleep in winter (children learned to play)

Arrangement

1

melothy of mixedness, the crane
chimney the crane, the craw, caw crow

call the caller (not), the guessed gone
livery of wanting, the goshawk, going, gone

the bird is (not), the bird sings, trill, coo
the trail is (not), walking, the toe

2

or boot and booted are (not) one
the rabbit's eye is (not) the gun

the styrofoam is (not) the cup
the leather grip is (not) the glove

the lovers' laugh is (not) a groan
a hunter's sighting is an end

3

beelzebub and flibberjab
one is insect, one is gab

one is mote in moter's aye
one is how to say good-bye

one a will is, one enough
cow and cat at water trough

4

water is as water does
clouding over, sliding down

winter is as water was
wavering the sculptured wind

wind and water weave a tone
wind and winter weave a bone

Visibility

1

sigh the dumb wick burnt
arrowed as of to ever spent

willow and wine a look annealed
flight to the roused nothing, once and was

the truce presented, now a now be were
the track annihilate, choke the bear bare

2

close the reminder, closeted book
choose, the closed book, clapping

clam and gentian reprobate, crotchety
steal at last look, asphodel, remain

sputter, and win and winnowed
rue is rue, unrailed, unravel ravel

3

bust and the lunatic spinner span
travel a stillness, travailed home

the kiss of breaking, teeth, tongue
toddle of losses, laughter laughed

and the holed mouth, mouthing
mouthed, mothermouth unmurmured

4

mesmerized by bane, moon mold
locket of moon, moonlack

but benny diction, loco as loquacious
loco is, cared emily, to interglade

the columbine, a carpet, dread dove
a mover, moved, a baser batter, bold

Figuration

1

the lost life last, we ewe ourselves
she we, astound the crittered riverbed

the wasn't us is all we are and sleep
the harpooned angel, and the crypt accuse

accost the apple and across the bow
home the hunter is, and well the crow

2

fallow the stubbled field, and and, alone
and coulees figurate the crisis wind

and call the dark birds down, the decoys dream
delay, the droning bees deliberate

delay descent, delay, and send the sky
the sky to kiss and elevate the eye

3

and toxic as the hemlock drink of old
the hunter take the cider and the cold

the epigram and eiderdown conclude
brooding and soft, the waders take to air

the willows rime, the far slough clamor call
and wear a noose of ice around its shore

4

delay, descending day, apostrophe
approve the call, the cliff of solitude

appearance peer, onto the glaze of what
is is or muted mood, the naked pot

tip down and clock unwind the winter tree
and sky and mallard fly the winter free

This Part of the Country

I. Kamloops: Late Arrival

Searching for the mountain,
we found a shoe.

After the first drought
we dreamed a river.
After the forecast city
we listened for rain.

The fallen roof and fireweed
conspire.
        Seeds too explode.

Iamb and jackhammer in duet:
silence, breaking the drum:
the city, climbing, climbing.

Two rivers, then, coming together.

2. This Part of the Country

In this part of the country, the horizon is a glacier.
One morning the horses of the sun lost all direction.

David Thompson, that very afternoon, found west. He saw
a man on a sandbar, sluicing for pieces of light.

I saw George Bowering riding a yellow horse, that high country poet
wearing no gun. His horse had eyes the color of bullets.

In this part of the country, sagebrush is a version of dance. You must
enter in slowly. This is where train robbers learn their moves.

I saw Roy Miki wading in Sheila Watson's river. He was fishing
with a line made of blue memory. The sky was tinder dry.

3. Blue River: Checking In

Somewhere west and south of Mt Robson
I forgot my name. This much I remember.
It was a long, white drive; I was alone.
The patient trees were shrouded in snow.

The woman behind the motel desk
said I would have to sign my name.
Snow had fallen, I explained, and it fell;
the road was not to be found.

We were both surprised by the dark.
Some days night is a voluntary silence.
Then one of us asked (was it she
or I?), So how did you get here?

4. This Part of the Country

Landscape is a diagram of the impossible. Why do we have to look at a tree to see the wind? How do we tell the frozen lake from future interrogations?

Today in Kamloops the snowline slid slowly all day long down into the valley of the North Thompson River. First my head turned a hummocky white. Then my shoulders became slopes for elegant white toboggans. Then all my fingers assumed the dignity of ice. It was a slow procedure. When I went to move my feet I couldn't find them.

Here in this part of the country the so-called visibility, from airplanes and avalanches alike, is the equivalent of zero. We measure our descent by exhalation, hoping to see each breath freeze as it escapes the mouth. Is that a question or an answer?

Acknowledgements

"Beached 3" appeared, under a different title, as the text in a print made by Tracy Jager and Gordon Trick at Coconut Monkey Press, Vancouver, British Columbia, in 2004.

The piece by Laura Kroetsch was published in the New Zealand literary journal, *Sport*. My daughter Laura lives Down Under. My daughter Megan lives in Florida.

"Lines Written in the John Snow House" appeared as a chapbook produced by housepress, Calgary, Alberta, in November, 2002. The characters in the poem are not fictitious. I wish to acknowledge and thank the following, in their order of appearance: Aritha van Herk, Dawne McCance , Nicole Markotic, Pauline Butling, Fred Wah, John Snow, Jackie Flanagan, Pamela Banting. My thanks also to Jackie Flanagan and Allan Markin and Derek Beaulieu for varieties of support.

"Poem for My Dead Sister" appeared in *A Likely Story: the writing life*, Red Deer College Press, Red Deer, Alberta, 1995. Again, a thank you to the publisher of that press, Dennis Johnson.

" This Part of the Country" appeared as a chapbook produced by Cariboo Bookworks Press, Kamloops, British Columbia, in March 2003. My thanks for plain old inspiration to Will Garrett-Petts and Donald Lawrence, and also to Roy Miki and George Bowering for their cameo appearances in the poem.

I wish to thank my agent Hilary McMahon of Westwood Creative Artists for her rare combination of patience and encouragement.

And once more, with admiration, my thanks to the people who make the University of Alberta Press such a unique and supportive publisher.

Other books by Robert Kroetsch
Published by The University of Alberta Press

What the Crow Said
Introduction by Robert R. Wilson
0-88864-303-9

The Words of My Roaring
Introduction by Thomas Wharton
0-88864-349-7

Completed Field Notes
The Long Poems of Robert Kroetsch
Introduction by Fred Wah
0-88864-350-0

The Hornbooks of Rita K
0-88864-372-1

The Studhorse Man
Introduction by Aritha van Herk
0-88864-425-6